Take Heart

Seven Apostolic Letters to Protect the Deposit of Faith

D1518244

Dedicated to my flock in Tyler, may God continue to watch over and protect you.

Table Of Contents

Foreword

It was the fourth watch of the night when Our Lord appeared to his disciples who were struggling to stay afloat. The sound of the cries from His terrified children immediately elicited those enduring words from the Savior; *"Take heart, it is I. Do not be afraid."*

The tripartite division of the night into three watches came from the Roman soldiers who took turns guarding their fellow brothers from any harm while they slept. If the night was longer a fourth watch would be added. The last watch, on the brink of *prima luce* was the hardest as the night is always darkest before the dawn of the new day. St. John Chrysostom underscored the significance of Christ waiting till the fourth watch, *"He suffers them to be tossed the whole night, exciting their hearts by fear, and inspiring them with greater desire and more lasting recollection of Him."*

This book, "Take Heart," arrives to the Catholic faithful at what seems like the fourth watch of the night. We are living in an unprecedented time of darkness and confusion. We have suffered through a very long night. Even the nocturnal guides of the moon and stars seem overshadowed by the clouds of confusing messages and deafening silence from Church leaders as the wolves of the secular world prey upon the sheep.

In the midst of this long night the first rosy fingered rays of dawn begin to appear. There is hope and signs of life all around. It is with great joy that I present to you one of these rays of light; Bishop Joseph Strickland's seven apostolic letters to Catholics examining the basic Truths of our Faith in these uniquely special times.

Bishop Strickland's letters are a reminder to us all of the beauty and richness of our Catholic faith, and how it can guide us through the complexities of this post-modern world. Through these letters, Bishop Strickland seeks to provide clear and compelling explanations of Catholic doctrine, and to inspire Catholics to embrace these teachings with renewed enthusiasm and commitment. He is unafraid to speak the truth, and his words are a powerful witness to the Gospel, and to the Deposit of Faith.

The officer that courageously rides a top his horse to inspire and lead his men as they charge across the battlefield becomes an instant focal point for direct fire. Bishop Strickland has most assuredly drawn that fire.

Knowing full well the fire that comes with standing by leaders who lead from the front we at Catholics for Catholics were absolutely honored when His Excellency asked us to publish this work. We have been blessed to work with Bishop Strickland. He will forever be in our hearts and memories for having attended our first ever Rosary Rally in June of 2023 when more than five thousand Catholics stood up for religious nuns AND WON outside Dodger Stadium.

The men and women of Catholics for Catholics run to the sound of bullets not away from them because that is who God called this organization to be. And most especially, we will step in to defend and support a Bishop, a Successor of the Apostles, for as my co-founder and dear friend Harold Ziegler Jr, frequently reminds me with his 90 years of wisdom; *'God came down to earth to establish the Catholic Church and therefore, it cannot be wrong. At the time, He gave the Apostles (Bishops) 100% jurisdiction to be responsible for growing the Church and keeping it from error. We are facing our greatest crisis ever, and so many Bishops stand in complicit silence as the Country and the Church fall apart.'*

We get out of bed in the morning excited to be Catholic. We also love our great country the United States of America. To be living through the fourth watch of a long night is exhilarating because our faith tells us to watch closely, for the Lord is coming soon walking upon the rough sea. Through His instruments, rays of light, like this book, will break the hold that the Prince of Darkness has been permitted to have.

As you read these letters, you will find yourself challenged and inspired. You will be encouraged to deepen your own faith, and to bring the light of Christ into the world around you. We encourage you wholeheartedly to share this with your family, friends, and clergy.

Our Lady also ran to the sound of bullets. Or rather, she ran to the Cross and stood with one of the first Bishops as they accompanied Our Lord in His Passion. She will also accompany us as we stand with our Bishops and Priests during this fourth watch of the night. With her we will hear the words of Christ and title of this book. "TAKE HEART!"

May God bless each of you and your families and we at Catholics for Catholics humbly ask for your prayers in return.

John C. Yep
CEO, Catholics for Catholics

December 8th, 2023
Feast of the Immaculate Conception,
Patroness of the United States of America

Introduction

August 22, 2023

My Dear Sons and Daughters in Christ:

May the love and grace of Our Lord Jesus Christ be upon you always! In this time of great turmoil in the Church and in the world, I must speak to you from a father's heart in order to warn you of the evils that threaten us, and to assure you of the joy and hope that we have always in our Lord Jesus Christ. The evil and false message that has invaded the Church, Christ's Bride, is that Jesus is only one among many, and that it is not necessary for His message to be shared with all humanity. This idea must be shunned and refuted at every turn. We must share the joyful good news that Jesus is our only Lord, and that He desires that all humanity for all time may embrace eternal life in Him.

Once we understand that Jesus Christ, God's Divine Son, is the fullness of revelation and the fulfillment of the Father's plan of salvation for all humanity for all time, and we embrace this with all our hearts, then we can address the other errors that plague our Church and our world which have been brought about by a departure from Truth.

In St. Paul's letter to the Galatians, he writes: "I am amazed that you are so quickly forsaking the one who called you by {the} grace {of Christ} for a different gospel {not that there is another}. But there are some who are disturbing you and wish to pervert the gospel of Christ. But even if we or an angel from heaven should preach {to you} a gospel other than the one that we preached to you, let that one be accursed! As we have said before, and now I say again, if anyone preaches to you a gospel other than the one that you received, let that one be accursed!" (Gal 1:6-9) As your spiritual father, I feel it is important to reiterate the following basic truths that have always been understood by the Church from time immemorial, and to emphasize that the Church exists not to redefine matters of faith, but to safeguard the Deposit of Faith as it has been handed down to us from Our Lord Himself through the apostles and the saints and martyrs. Again, hearkening back to St. Paul's warning to the Galatians, any attempts to pervert the true Gospel message must be categorically rejected as injurious to the Bride of Christ and her individual members.

1. Christ established One Church—the Catholic Church—and, therefore, only the Catholic Church provides the fullness of Christ's truth and the authentic path to His salvation for all of us.
2. The Eucharist and all the sacraments are divinely instituted, not developed by man. The Eucharist is truly Christ's Body and Blood, Soul and Divinity, and to receive Him in Communion unworthily (i.e. in a state of grave, unrepentant sin) is a devastating sacrilege for the individual and for the Church. (1 Cor 11:27-29)
3. The Sacrament of Matrimony is instituted by God. Through Natural Law, God has established marriage as between one man and one woman faithful to each other for life and open to children. Humanity has no right or true ability to redefine marriage.
4. Every human person is created in the image and likeness of God, male or female, and all people should be helped to discover their true identities as children of God, and not supported in a disordered attempt to reject their undeniable biological and God-given identity.
5. Sexual activity outside marriage is always gravely sinful and cannot be condoned, blessed, or deemed permissible by any authority inside the Church.
6. The belief that all men and women will be saved regardless of how they live their lives (a concept commonly referred to as universalism) is false and is dangerous, as it contradicts what Jesus tells us repeatedly in the Gospel. Jesus says we must "deny ourselves, take up our cross and follow Him." (Matt 16:24) He has given us the way, through His grace, to victory over sin and death through repentance and sacramental confession. It is essential that we embrace the joy and hope, as well as the freedom, that come from repentance and humbly confessing our sins. Through repentance and sacramental confession, every battle with temptation and sin can be a small victory that leads us to embrace the great victory that Christ has won for us.

7. In order to follow Jesus Christ, we must willingly choose to take up our cross instead of attempting to avoid the cross and suffering that Our Lord offers to each of us individually in our daily lives. The mystery of redemptive suffering—i.e. suffering that Our Lord allows us to experience and accept in this world and then offer back to Him in union with His suffering—humbles us, purifies us, and draws us deeper into the joy of a life lived in Christ. That is not to say that we must enjoy or seek out suffering, but if we are united to Christ, as we experience our daily sufferings we can find the hope and joy that exist amidst the suffering and persevere to the end in all our suffering. (cf. 2 Tim 4:6-8)

In the weeks and months ahead, many of these truths will be examined as part of the Synod on Synodality. We must hold fast to these truths and be wary of any attempts to present an alternative to the Gospel of Jesus Christ, or to push for a faith that speaks of dialogue and brotherhood, while attempting to remove the fatherhood of God. When we seek to innovate upon what God in His great mercy has given us, we find ourselves upon treacherous ground. The surest footing we can find is to remain firmly upon the perennial teachings of the faith.

Regrettably, it may be that some will label as schismatics those who disagree with the changes being proposed. Be assured, however, that no one who remains firmly upon the plumb line of our Catholic faith is a schismatic. We must remain unabashedly and truly Catholic, regardless of what may be brought forth. We must be aware also that it is not leaving the Church to stand firm against these proposed changes. As St. Peter said, "Lord to whom shall we go? You have the words of eternal life." (Jn 6:68) Therefore, standing firm does not mean we are seeking to leave the Church. Instead, those who would propose changes to that which cannot be changed seek to commandeer Christ's Church, and they are indeed the true schismatics.

I urge you, my sons and daughters in Christ, that now is the time to make sure you stand firmly upon the Catholic faith of the ages. We were all created to seek the Way, the Truth and the Life, and in this modern age of confusion, the true path is the one that is illuminated by the light of Jesus Christ, for Truth has a face and indeed it is His face. Be assured that He will not abandon His Bride.

I remain your humble father and servant,

Most Reverend Joseph E. Strickland
Bishop of Tyler

The Nature of The Church

September 5, 2023

My Dear Sons and Daughters in Christ:

I write to you today to discuss more fully the first basic truth that I spoke of in my first pastoral letter: "Christ established One Church—the Catholic Church—and, therefore, only the Catholic Church provides the fullness of Christ's truth and the authentic path to His salvation for all of us."

To begin, I must state clearly and emphatically this fundamental truth—Jesus Christ is the only path to everlasting life; no other path to salvation can be found! As Our Lord Himself tells us: "I am the way and the truth and the life. No one comes to the Father except through Me." (Jn 14:6). In order that we might participate in that promise of everlasting life, Our Lord in His great mercy established the One, Holy, Catholic, and Apostolic Church. As we read in the Gospel of Matthew, Christ said: "And so I say to you, you are Peter, and upon this rock I will build my church, and the gates of the netherworld shall not prevail against it. I will give you the keys to the kingdom of heaven. Whatever you bind on earth shall be bound in heaven; and whatever you loose on earth shall be loosed in heaven." (Matt 16:18-19). The foundation and divine head of the Church is Jesus Christ; however, this passage makes it clear that Jesus is promising to establish a visible Church upon the earth with a visible head, Peter, to whom He will entrust a unique mission and a specific authority.

The Catholic Church IS the body of Christ, and He is inseparable from His body. The Church's understanding of Christ's words in Matthew has deepened throughout the ages, but in accordance with Sacred Tradition handed down from

Christ to the Apostles (cf. 2 Thess 2:15), and then preserved and protected by the Church Fathers and saints and martyrs until today, it has always been understood and proclaimed that the Catholic Church is the single, divinely-instituted Church that Christ established for the salvation of souls. All that the Church is, as the mystical body of Christ, flows from the truth that it was, and is, divinely constituted by Christ, and her basic elements—which include the sacred Deposit of Faith—cannot be altered by men because it does not belong to men; the Church belongs to Christ!

St. Cyril of Jerusalem stated in A.D. 350: "The Church is called catholic then because it extends over all the world, from one end of the earth to the other; and because it teaches universally and completely the doctrines that ought to come to men's knowledge, concerning things both visible and invisible, heavenly and earthly; and because it brings into subjection to godliness the whole race of mankind, governors and governed, learned and unlearned; and because it universally treats and heals the whole class of sins that are committed by soul or body, and possesses in itself every form of virtue that is named, both in deeds and words, and in every spiritual gift."

Christ therefore established His Church for all people, for all time, for the salvation of all. There is no salvation apart from Christ and His One, Holy, Catholic, and Apostolic Church; this is an infallible teaching of the Church. However, as the Catechism of the Catholic Church states, "This affirmation is not aimed at those who, through no fault of their own, do not know Christ and His Church." As Catholics, we are lovingly and joyfully bound to the Church and to the seven sacraments instituted by Christ. These are essential for our salvation. Some may ask, however: "What about those outside the Church? What about those who have never heard of Christ? Can they be saved?" For those who are not united to Christ through His Church and through the grace of the sacraments, we simply pray for them and entrust them to God. Although we must never be presumptuous of God's grace, we recognize that God is sovereign, and if in His mercy He would choose to operate in ways beyond our knowledge or understanding, He has full authority to operate however He chooses because He is not bound by anything other than His own perfect nature.

We ourselves must cling tightly to the Church and the sacraments as He gave them to us, but we must also pray always for souls outside the Church, that God offers His grace to those souls in ways unknown and unseen to us. However, I want to emphasize this point—if God would choose to offer grace beyond the normal sacramental means, we recognize that this grace would always still flow to

5

every soul from Christ and through His Church in a mystical way. Therefore, anyone receiving and accepting God's grace would never be saved through any other path or church or religion; there is One Savior, One Redeemer, for all mankind, and He established One Church for the salvation of souls.

God desires the salvation of all, but He does not force salvation upon any of us; it requires our cooperation and free assent to His grace. He calls each one of us to participate in His plan of salvation not only for ourselves, but for the world; this is the Great Commission: "Go, therefore, and make disciples of all nations, baptizing them in the name of the Father, and of the Son, and of the Holy Spirit, teaching them to observe all that I have commanded you. And behold, I am with you always, until the end of the age." (Matt 28:19-20).

We live in an age of great interconnectedness where people across the globe can share and learn with each other as never before in human history. This is a great blessing in many respects as it opens the possibility of sharing the Good News of Jesus Christ in ways not before possible. True ecumenism, however, is an open invitation to all people to experience and embrace the fullness of Christ and the Christian life which can be found only in the Catholic Church. This path, although difficult at times, is the only sure path to true everlasting love, grace, and life with God. It is false charity to tell people that regardless of what path they are on, it is God's Will that they stay where they are because this does not call on people to embrace the one true path instituted by God for the salvation of souls. Therefore, the Church has a sacred obligation, borne of love, to evangelize all people.

Another topic that I want to discuss because it will reportedly be a topic of discussion at the upcoming Synod on Synodality is the divinely-instituted structure of the Church as it applies to ordination of women. As Sacred Scripture tells us, Christ ordained only men as apostles. Sacred Tradition and the Ordinary Magisterium of the Church have affirmed throughout the ages that the Church has no authority whatsoever to ordain women to the priesthood. This cannot be changed because Christ instituted a male priesthood in order to image Himself as the bridegroom with the Church as His bride. As St. John Paul II solemnly stated in his apostolic letter *Ordinatio Sacerdotalis*: "I declare that the Church has no authority whatsoever to confer priestly ordination on women and that this judgment is to be definitively held by all the Church's faithful."

It is imperative to state, though, that Christ would never want a "lesser" role for women than He wants for men. Women have made and continue to make indispensable contributions in the history and life of the Church. From the greatest and most perfect of God's creation in all of history, Our Blessed Mother, the Queen of Heaven and Earth; to some of the greatest saints and Doctors of the Church; to our holy and faithful women in religious orders and convents; to the countless women who have and continue to impart the faith to their families and communities; Christ instituted His Church in a way that calls for women to have "more" of a role in Him than could ever be found in the world. However, as God did not call men to be mothers, God did not call women to be fathers, and to be sacramentally ordained as a minister for Christ in His Church, Our Lord calls for men to be spiritual fathers and bridegrooms to His bride, The Church. This role can only be filled by one properly ordered to this role.

For those who would inquire about the potential for female deacons in the Catholic Church, I would offer this: Scripture tells us that from the earliest days of the Church, women served as faithful servants (Greek: *diakonos*) of the members of the Church. (cf. Rom 16:1). Historians and scholars tell us that women served in many important roles of service in the early Church, including acts of charity for the poor, caring for the sick, preparing other women for baptism, etc. However, we see in the Acts of the Apostles that there is another type of servant (*diakonos*) called specifically by the apostles and set apart from other servants in the Church; the apostles laid hands on these particular servants, and these servants then received a sacramental ordination to fulfill their unique role. Scripture tells us that the apostles said, "Brothers, select from among you seven reputable men, filled with the Spirit and wisdom, who we appoint to this task." (Acts 6:3). And then, "They presented these men to the apostles who prayed and laid hands on them." (Acts 6:6). Although many (both men and women) have faithfully served the Church as servants/*diakonos* throughout history, the sacramental ordination to the diaconate—as one of the three degrees of the sacrament of Holy Orders (deacon, priest, bishop)—has always been reserved for baptized males alone. All three degrees act as instruments of Christ *in persona Christi Capitis,* (in the person of Christ as the Head), but with distinct functions for each office. Because sacramentally ordained deacons share in the apostolic ministry with priests and bishops, the Church has decreed that they must also be men, as were the apostles Jesus chose.

The Canons of the Council of Nicaea (A.D. 325) state in reference to women who have been granted a certain status of service: "We refer to deaconesses who have been granted this status, for they do not receive any imposition of hands, so that they are in all respects to be numbered among the laity." (Canon No. 19).

In conclusion, I want to state that although the Church is holy because of her Founder and her divine origin, she is also made up of sinful members who are called constantly to repentance and conversion. However, there is a Church Triumphant in heaven that exists perfectly in her fullness in Christ in heaven where the heavenly marriage feast is eternally celebrated with God—Father, Son, and Holy Spirit—who are eternally worshipped and adored. The choirs of angels, the Immaculate Virgin Mary, and all the saints eternally cry "Holy, Holy, Holy" before the throne of God.

It is important that we, as the Church Militant on earth, carry this truth and hope in our hearts as we strive to align ourselves and every aspect of the Church on this earth with her heavenly reality. Because of sin, both personal and communal, the Church Militant on earth falls short of the Church Triumphant in heaven, but it is our mission to strive always for holiness and by the grace of God to persevere until the end so that we might also join with the Church Triumphant. Part of this striving on earth consists in engaging in the spiritual battle that is taking place around us daily as many attempt to chip away or destroy altogether the Deposit of Faith.

My dear sons and daughters, be assured that angels surround us in this battle, and saints—especially Our Holy and Blessed Mother—offer their heavenly assistance as we seek the eternal prize Our Lord has won for us.

Remaining your humble father and servant,

Most Reverend Joseph E. Strickland
Bishop of Tyler, Texas

The Eucharist

September 12, 2023

My Dear Sons and Daughters in Christ:

I write to you today to discuss more fully the second basic truth that I spoke of in my first pastoral letter issued on August 22, 2023: "The Eucharist and all the sacraments are divinely instituted, not developed by man. The Eucharist is truly Christ's Body and Blood, Soul and Divinity, and to receive Him in Communion unworthily (i.e. in a state of grave, unrepentant sin) is a devastating sacrilege for the individual and for the Church." (1 Cor 11:27-29).

The sacraments are essential elements of the fullness of life in Christ and are, above all, a divine love story. The sacraments are channels of God's divine grace which flow from Christ Himself, love incarnate among us, and sanctify each of us on our journey towards Heaven. They are visible signs of God's love for us. Through worthy reception of the sacraments, God's supernatural grace is brought forth in visible and tangible form, and the work of God's salvation is made manifest in each of us. As the Catechism of the Catholic Church states: "The sacraments are efficacious signs of grace, instituted by Christ and entrusted to the Church, by which divine life is dispensed to us. The visible rites by which the sacraments are celebrated signify and make present the graces proper to each sacrament. They bear fruit in those who receive them with the required dispositions." (CCC 1131).

There are seven sacraments of the Catholic Church: Baptism, Confirmation, Eucharist, Reconciliation (Confession), Anointing of the Sick, Matrimony, and Holy Orders. The sacraments are not isolated from one another but instead are woven together in a unity of divine life that reflects and connects us to the ministry of Jesus Christ and His Church. The saints and Doctors of the Church have given us many beautiful reflections to ponder regarding the origin of the sacraments. St. Thomas Aquinas said that from the pierced side of Christ "flowed forth the sacraments of the Church, without which there is no entrance to the life which is the true life. That blood was shed for the remission of sins; that water it is that makes up the health-giving cup."

The Eucharist is at the very center of our sacramental life because the Eucharist IS the Real Presence of Christ Himself. It is my intent in this letter to speak mainly of the Eucharist, and the importance of not receiving Our Lord in Communion unworthily. I will discuss the remaining sacraments in more detail in future pastoral letters.

The Eucharist: Simply put, the Eucharist is the source and summit of the Christian life. It is the Body and Blood, Soul and Divinity of our Lord Jesus Christ—His Real Presence among us. When we consume the Eucharist, we are incorporated into Christ in a supernatural way, and we are also bound to all others who are of the Body of Christ.

Holy Communion is an intimate encounter with Jesus Christ. Jesus said, "Amen, amen, I say to you, unless you eat the flesh of the Son of Man and drink his blood, you do not have life within you. Whoever eats my flesh and drinks my blood has eternal life, and I will raise him on the last day. For my flesh is true food, and my blood is true drink. Whoever eats my flesh and drinks my blood remains in me and I in him. Just as the living Father sent me and I have life because of the Father, so also the one who feeds on me will have life because of me. This is the bread that came down from heaven. Unlike your ancestors who ate and still died, whoever eats this bread will live forever." (Jn 6:53-58).

One of the countless stories from the history of the Church provides a beautiful message of the power of the Eucharist. St. Damien of Molokai, a Belgian priest in the mid-19th century, was sent to the missionary fields of Hawaii where he would spend his life in the care and service of those who were afflicted with leprosy. For many years, St. Damien loved and took care of the leper colony single-handedly, tending to the physical and spiritual needs of all in the community. One might wonder what could have given him the spiritual strength for such a difficult and heart-wrenching mission, a mission that ended with his contracting and dying from the disease himself. St. Damien gives us the answer; he said it was the Eucharist. St. Damien wrote, "Were it not for the constant presence of our Divine Master in our humble chapel, I would not have found it possible to persevere in sharing the lot of the afflicted in Molokai … The Eucharist is the bread that gives strength … It is at once the most eloquent proof of His love and the most powerful means of fostering His love in us. He gives Himself every day so that our hearts as burning coals may set afire the hearts of the faithful." The Eucharist was St. Damien's spiritual strength, and the Lord wants it to be our strength as well.

Living a sacramental life as members of the Catholic Church, the mystical Body of Christ, hinges on belief in the Real Presence of Jesus Christ in the Eucharist. From the very beginning of the Church until today, saints and martyrs have lived and died for their belief in the Real Presence; kings and commoners have knelt side by side in their belief in the Real Presence; and countless Eucharistic miracles throughout the world continue to testify to Our Lord's Real Presence in the Eucharist. Throughout the ages, the Church came to a deeper and more profound understanding of this sacred mystery which we now know as the dogma of transubstantiation. Transubstantiation is the word the Church uses to describe the change that takes place at each mass when the priest pronounces the words of consecration: "This is my Body." "This is My Blood." When these sacred words are spoken by the priest, the substance of the bread and wine are transformed by Our Lord into His body and blood, and only the appearances (that is, the physical properties) of bread and wine remain. Our senses cannot perceive this change, but at this sacred moment when Heaven and Earth meet, the risen Christ is truly made present for us in every mass, just as He told us He would be: "And behold, I am with you always, until the end of the age." (Matt 28:20).

As Catholics, we are joyfully bound to believe that Christ is truly present in the Eucharist.

In his first letter to the Corinthians, St. Paul tells us: "Therefore whoever eats the bread or drinks the cup of the Lord unworthily will have to answer for the body and blood of the Lord. A person should examine himself, and so eat the bread and drink the cup. For anyone who eats and drinks without discerning the body, eats and drinks judgment on himself." (1 Cor 11:27-29).

We pray at every Mass immediately before receiving the Body of Christ in Communion, "Lord, I am not worthy that you should enter under my roof, but only say the word and my soul shall be healed." As we pray this prayer, we acknowledge that we are all sinners and therefore unworthy to receive the Body and Blood of the Lord of our own accord, but we acknowledge that His supreme work of mercy makes us worthy—if we choose to accept His grace and conform our lives to His. The essential call is for all of us individually to do our best to seek holiness and to ensure that any mortal sin of which we are conscious has been sacramentally confessed prior to receiving Holy Communion. To receive the Eucharist while ignoring unrepented mortal sin in our lives or without discerning Our Lord's Real Presence brings spiritual destruction rather than a deeper life in Christ.

A mortal sin is any sin whose matter is grave and which has been committed willfully and with full knowledge of its seriousness. These grave matters include (but are not limited to): murder, receiving or participating in abortion, homosexual acts, sexual intercourse outside marriage or in an invalid marriage, deliberately engaging in impure thoughts, the use of contraception, etc. If you have questions regarding sins or the need for sacramental confession, I urge you to talk to your parish priest; and if you have committed a mortal sin, I implore you to go to confession before receiving the Eucharist.

The 1983 Code of Canon Law states, "A person who is conscious of a grave sin is not to ... receive the body of the Lord without prior sacramental confession unless a grave reason is present and there is no opportunity of confession; in this case the person is to be mindful of the obligation to make an act of perfect contrition, including the intention of confessing as soon as possible." (CIC 916). This teaching is also found in the Didache, an early Christian document dating from around A.D. 70. These documents, written almost 2,000 years apart, highlight the Church's constant understanding of the importance of being aware of our sins and seeking sacramental confession when it is needed. If we intentionally live in a manner which runs contrary to the teaching of the Catholic faith, and we obstinately hold to beliefs that contradict the truth which the Church teaches, we place ourselves in a state of grave spiritual danger. We can take comfort that this can be remedied since God's abundant mercy is always available to us, but we must humbly repent and confess our sins to receive His forgiveness.

This brings me to another point I would like to discuss since it is likely to be discussed at the upcoming Synod on Synodality. There has been much discussion regarding individuals who self-identify as members of the LGBTQ community who seek to receive Holy Communion. I feel it is important to state the following in this pastoral letter: The Church offers love and friendship to all LGBTQ individuals, as Christ offers to each one of us, and the Church seeks to enable every person to live out the authentic call to holiness that God intends for them. We must be clear, however, that the Church cannot offer a person Holy Communion if that person is actively engaging in a same-sex relationship, or if a person is not living as the sex that God formed them to be at their conception and birth. The Church teaches that those who experience feelings of same-sex attraction or gender dysphoria do not sin simply because they have such feelings, but freely acting upon those feelings is sinful and not in accordance with God's design for His children. For those who experience these feelings, it is indeed a difficult path so I encourage you to seek the spiritual and emotional support of your parish priest and of family and friends of faith who can help you to discern and live out the authentic call to holiness God intends for you. I would also offer this—regardless of who we are, we must always remember that following Jesus means following the way of the Cross. It will be difficult, but rest assured, He walks it with us if we ask Him.

Additionally, I want to state clearly that the Church has never and will never condone the reception of the Eucharist by a Catholic who persists in any adulterous union. A person must first repent of the sin of adultery and receive sacramental absolution, and also have the firm resolution to avoid this sin in the future. In other words, the adultery must end for the individual to receive Holy Communion. For those who may have been in a previous marriage and have divorced and now seek to remarry, I would urge you to speak to your parish priest so he may advise and assist you in your specific situation.

As part of the Body of Christ, we must remember that all people are children of God; Christ shed His blood for each and every person. We love and welcome our non-Catholic brothers and sisters, and we should seek to invite them into the fullness of the One, Holy, Catholic, and Apostolic Church whenever possible. I encourage you to share your faith and invite them to attend Holy Mass with you, even though they are unable to receive Communion. As part of sharing your faith, I ask that you share with them why the Eucharist is so special and why it is reserved only for Catholics who are in a state of grace (without mortal sin) and who are in full communion with the Church.

There is no shortage of great saints who spoke and wrote eloquently about the beauty, power, and spiritual efficacy of the Eucharist, from early Church Fathers such as St. Justin Martyr and St. Ignatius of Antioch, to Doctors of the Church such as St. Augustine and St. Thomas Aquinas, to saints of more modern times such as St. Peter Julian Eymard and Pope St. Pius X. I encourage all to make a commitment to learn from faithful saints such as these in order to deepen our love and appreciation of our Eucharistic Lord who gave His Body and Blood, Soul and Divinity in a perfect sacrifice for the salvation of the world.

The beauty of the sacraments, especially the Eucharist, calls us to an ever-deepening relationship with Jesus Christ, living and present among us. Let us seek a more profound faith that Jesus Christ who walked among us two thousand years ago remains with us as He promised. The sacraments are Christ among us, calling us to live His sacrificial love in all our interactions with other members of His Body the Church.

May Our Lord bless you and may Our Blessed Mother intercede for you as you continue to grow in faith, hope and charity.

Remaining your humble father and servant,

Most Reverend Joseph E. Strickland
Bishop of Tyler, Texas

Matrimony and Holy Orders

September 19th, 2023

My Dear Sons and Daughters in Christ:

I write to you today to discuss more fully the third basic truth that I spoke of in my first pastoral letter issued on August 22, 2023: "The sacrament of Matrimony is instituted by God. Through Natural Law, God has established marriage as between one man and one woman faithful to each other for life and open to children. (CCC 1601). Humanity has no right or true ability to redefine marriage."

In addition to the sacrament of Matrimony, I will also discuss the sacrament of Holy Orders in this letter, as both Matrimony and Holy Orders are vocations and are, therefore, calls from Our Lord to share our lives with others in special ways. Both Matrimony and Holy Orders confer a special grace that is primarily directed not towards the salvation of the one who receives the sacrament, but in particular towards the salvation of those who are served by the one married or ordained. Thus, both are properly understood as sacraments of service. In both cases the fundamental aspect, as intended by God, is a self-sacrificial love that wills the sanctification of the beloved.

Matrimony: According to the Catechism of the Council of Trent, "marriage is a conjugal union between a man and a woman, both in legal status, in which they establish a perpetual and indissoluble union of lives. There are two goals in this union—procreation and education of the offspring, and the mutual support of the spouses." This definition is applicable to both marriage between two non-baptized people, and marriage between two baptized people. In the first, the marriage is contracted according to Natural Law, and in the second, the marriage is contracted according to the Church and is fortified by sacramental graces.

Let us look specifically at three major buildings blocks of marriage. First, let us look at the definition of marriage as being between one man and one woman. We can turn to the initial chapters of the book of Genesis for the clear revelation that marriage between one man and one woman is ordained by God for the proper ordering of humanity. "The Lord God said: 'It is not good for the man to be alone. I will make a helper suited to him.'" (Gen 2:18). And then, "So the Lord God cast a deep sleep on the man, and while he was asleep, he took out one of his ribs and closed up its place with flesh. The Lord God then built the rib that he had taken from the man into a woman. When he brought her to the man, the man said: 'This one, at last, is bone of my bones and flesh of my flesh; This one shall be called woman, for out of man this one has been taken.'" (Gen 2:21-23) Because marriage was divinely instituted by God as between one man and one woman, there is simply no right given to humanity to depart from this foundational truth of marriage. I will reemphasize this point: marriage can only be between one man and one woman. Our global society has entered gravely dangerous territory as it promotes various distortions of intimate human relationships and attempts to label them as "marriage." These models are not rooted in the truth which God has revealed to us in Sacred Scripture and which is woven into Natural Law, and we are seeing the sad fruits of these denials of God's divine blueprint for marriage.

The second building block of marriage is that it is meant to be a lifetime commitment—a perpetual and indissoluble union of two lives united together in a life-long covenant. Marriages that end in divorce and thus fail to fulfill the call of an enduring bond cause havoc not only in the lives of each member of the broken family, but also in society. Compassion compels us to pray for those who have experienced broken marriages that God's grace may bring healing, forgiveness, and wholeness; but we recognize that the pain and upheaval brought about from the breakdown of the marriage testify to the necessity of marriage as a permanent and unbreakable covenant. If one or both of the parties enter a marriage lacking this firm resolution for permanence, it can spell disaster for this union, and it also calls into question whether a true marriage has taken place because an essential element was missing from the beginning.

Finally, we turn to the third building block of marriage, that it is to be open to children. The Church in her wisdom, guided by Sacred Tradition, does not claim that a childless marriage is not a true marriage. The point which the Church insists on, however, is that there must be an openness to children in the marriage. The prevalent use of contraception even among believing Catholics undermines this third essential building block of marriage in devastating ways. It is crucial that we address this issue with the gravity that it demands.

In these current times, the Catholic Church seems to stand virtually alone in opposing contraception because the Church has always recognized that contraception runs contrary to God's plan for human life, and that cannot and will not change. Prior to 1930, virtually every other Christian community also stood in opposition to the use of contraception as a gravely sinful act. In 1930 at the Lambeth Conference, the Anglican Communion declared that married couples, for serious reasons, could use artificial contraception. It was not long after this that numerous other Protestant denominations also approved the use of contraception. However, the Catholic Church held firm that artificial contraception was, is, and forever will be gravely sinful.

On New Year's Eve 1930, the Church officially responded to those who argued in favor of contraception by the release of Pope Pius XI's encyclical on marriage, *Casti Connubii*. This encyclical clearly reiterated that the use of any "artificial" means of birth control was prohibited because it interfered with God's design for human life, and therefore was a mortal sin. "Since, therefore, openly departing from the uninterrupted Christian tradition some recently have judged it possible solemnly to declare another doctrine regarding this question, the Catholic Church, to whom God has entrusted the defense of the integrity and purity of morals, standing erect in the midst of the moral ruin which surrounds her, in order that she may preserve the chastity of the nuptial union from being defiled by this foul stain, raises her voice in token of her divine ambassadorship and through Our mouth proclaims anew: any use whatsoever of matrimony exercised in such a way that the act is deliberately frustrated in its natural power to generate life is an offense against the law of God and of nature, and those who indulge in such are branded with the guilt of a grave sin." (Casti Connubii, para. 56).

In the 1960's, the invention of the birth control pill gave rise to the so-called "sexual revolution." The majority of women who wanted to thwart their natural fertility now turned to the birth control pill. However, most women, then as now, were not aware that birth control pills have an abortifacient component— meaning these pills can and do cause the termination of a fertilized ovum, a conceived child, as one of their functions. Birth control pills do three things: they thicken cervical mucus; they inhibit ovulation; and in the event of fertilization, they block implantation of the fertilized ovum, making them abortifacient in nature. The connection between birth control and abortion was intentionally downplayed by birth control advocates in order to bring less scrutiny of hormonal contraceptives. However, we as Catholics must understand that the use of such drugs could actually cause a conceived child to be aborted before a woman even knew she was carrying a child. As children of God made in His image and likeness, we are called to honor and respect each human being from conception until natural death. Contraception stands in the way of this, and therefore Catholics must reject the use of hormonal contraceptives as gravely sinful.

Regarding abortion, the Catechism of the Catholic Church states, "Since the first century the Church has affirmed the moral evil of every procured abortion. This teaching has not changed and remains unchangeable. Direct abortion, that is to say, abortion willed either as an end or a means, is gravely contrary to the moral law." (CCC 2271). Modern science has not changed the Church's teaching against abortion, but instead has confirmed that the life of each individual begins with the earliest zygote and embryo. Because each and every human life has inherent dignity, each life must be treated with respect.

I would like to focus now on the importance of marriage as a sacrament, a sign of God's grace at work in the world. A marriage is sacramental when it is validly celebrated between a baptized man and a baptized woman. Matrimony is the one sacrament that the participants confer on one another. This sacramental reality encompasses all the elements of a natural marriage and adds to it the beauty of a vocation lived out before God, with His grace given to the husband and wife to live out that vocation. Just as natural marriage is foundational for human civilization, sacramental marriage is essential for the life of the Church. The grace that flows into the lives of a man and a woman in a sacramental marriage also flows out from their union as a blessing for their family and their community. Sacramental marriage reaps the blessing from graces which allow the man and woman, along with any children they are blessed to nurture, to form a domestic Church and to live out their unique call to holiness in their family as directed by God. For the Church to accomplish her mission of bringing Christ to the world, holy sacramental marriages are essential.

As we approach the upcoming Synod on Synodality, we must continue to hold fast to Sacred Scripture, the Sacred Traditions of the Church, and the unchangeable Deposit of Faith which illumine and guide our faith regarding Matrimony. We must be aware of and reject any call for a change in the unchangeable reality of marriage, and we must also reject any call for recognition or blessings on relationships which attempt to simulate or redefine the sacrament of Matrimony. Any relationship that is not a true marriage but attempts to portray itself as a true marriage is a deception that would inevitably lead souls away from Christ and into the hands of the deceiver. As your spiritual father, I must caution you in the strongest terms—do not accept this deception.

In conclusion of our discussion regarding matrimony, we must recognize just how far modern society has slipped from the covenantal, life-giving concept of Holy Matrimony as given by God. As homosexual relationships are more and more recognized throughout the world as "marriages"; as marriages in many cases are believed to be "disposable" through the widespread presence of divorce; as contraception is now widely used, even by Catholics; and as abortion is not only permitted, but celebrated throughout our country and our world; the very fabric of marriage is being ripped apart at the seams.

From Pope Pius XI: "Yet not only do We, looking with paternal eye on the universal world from this Apostolic See as from a watchtower, but you, also, Venerable Brethren, see, and seeing deeply grieve with Us that a great number of men, forgetful of the divine work of redemption, either entirely ignore or shamelessly deny the great sanctity of Christian wedlock, or relying on the false principles of a new and utterly perverse morality, too often trample it under foot. And since these most pernicious errors and depraved morals have begun to spread even amongst the faithful and are gradually gaining ground, in Our office as Christ's Vicar upon earth and Supreme Shepherd and Teacher, We consider it our duty to raise Our voice to keep the flock committed to Our care from poisoned pastures and, as far as in Us lies, to preserve it from harm" (Casti Connubii, para. 3).

Holy Orders: "No one has a right to receive the sacrament of Holy Orders. Indeed no one claims this office for himself; he is called to it by God." (CCC 1578). "Holy Orders is the sacrament through which the mission entrusted by Christ to his apostles continues to be exercised in the Church until the end of time: thus it is the sacrament of apostolic ministry. It includes three degrees: episcopate, presbyterate, and diaconate." (CCC 1536). Ordination is a sacramental act in which a man is integrated into the order of bishops, presbyters (priests), or deacons, and it confers the gift of the Holy Spirit that permits the exercise of a "sacred power" which comes from Christ Himself. In ordination, the bishop lays hands on the one being ordained and offers a prayer of consecration. These are the visible signs of the sacrament. In the sacrament of Baptism, all the faithful share in the common priesthood of Christ. However, in the sacrament of Holy Orders, a priest's participation in Christ's ministry differs from the common priesthood of the faithful as it confers the power to serve in the name and in the person of Christ (*in persona Christi*).

Pope Pius XI, in his encyclical *Ad Catholici Sacerdotii*, gives many beautiful explanations of the holiness of a priestly vocation. An essential thread echoes the self-sacrificial character we noted earlier when discussing marriage, but in the case of the priest, it is even more so a complete reliance upon and full abandonment of one's life to God. As Pius XI beautifully states, "A priest is one who should be totally dedicated to the things of the Lord. Is it not right, then, that he be entirely detached from the things of the world, and have his conversation in Heaven? A priest's charge is to be solicitous for the eternal salvation of souls, continuing in their regard the work of the Redeemer. Is it not, then, fitting that he keeps himself free from the cares of a family, which would absorb a great part of his energies?" (Ad Catholici Sacerdotii, para. 45). This statement also highlights the reason for priestly celibacy. The priest is called to forego, on the natural level, a human family (i.e., marriage and children) in order to espouse on a supernatural level the Church in his role as "*alter Christus*." Following the example of Our Lord, the priest is to make of his life a complete sacrifice for the sanctification of souls, up to and including the shedding of his blood—thereby participating in the bringing forth of new life, but on the supernatural level.

The priest never serves on his own behalf. Without priests, the Church would be without the Eucharist. Pope St. John Paul II stated, "There can be no Eucharist without the priesthood, just as there can be no priesthood without the Eucharist."

The road of the priest is the cross, and he must embrace it fully and lovingly. It is not enough to simply believe in Our Lord, because martyrdom is more than simply the action of one who believes; it is the action of one who loves. From the first priests—the Apostles themselves—to countless examples of extraordinary acts of heroism from seeming ordinary men such as Blessed Fr. Stanley Rother, Blessed Fr. Jerzy Popiełuszko, and Servant of God Fr. Emil Kapaun, Our Lord has been abundant in generously gifting His Bride the Church throughout the centuries with priests who answered the ultimate call to love—not through their own power—but through the work of the Holy Spirit within their souls. Yet, for the vast majority of priests, the martyrdom they are presented with may not be as dramatic as the shedding of blood. It may be that they are offered the crown of white martyrdom, of daily picking up their crosses and shepherding their flocks with love through the everyday trials and tribulations that plague fallen humanity. Humility and abandonment of course are paramount; the priest must make his life a gift to Our Lord to direct as He wills, and the greater the level of abandonment, the greater the gift. That is the nature of love.

It is through the sacrament of Holy Orders that God calls and then equips deacons, priests, and bishops to serve His people, to minister to them, to teach them, and to sanctify them so that His people may have a sure path to holiness and to receiving the salvation that Christ has won for each person. In order to carry out these roles, however, we must remember that it is God who calls His chosen instruments to the sacrament of Holy Orders, and the Church who confirms the call.

As we approach the Synod on Synodality, we must remember that God would never call a person to a role which they were not able to fulfill. As I stated in my pastoral letter from September 5, 2023, Sacred Tradition and the Ordinary Magisterium of the Church have affirmed throughout the ages that the Church has no authority whatsoever to ordain women, as Christ called those who would minister in His Name to image Himself as the bridegroom with the Church as His bride. Because the Church has no authority to ordain women, we recognize that God would never authentically call a woman to the sacrament of Holy Orders. As such, if any were to suggest a change could be made to this sacred and unchangeable doctrine, we must recognize this as a break from the Deposit of Faith and reject the idea as contrary to the faith.

In conclusion I would like to say to you, my dear sons and daughters in Christ, do not despair. It is evident when we look back through salvation history that any time humanity moves away from God, He pours out an abundance of divine grace upon the faithful so that His children may return to Him. God is depending on each of us to help lead humanity back to Himself; let us meet Him in Mass, in the sacraments, in prayer, and in Eucharistic adoration. We are all called to participate in His divine plan of salvation, and so we must proclaim as did St. Joan of Arc, "I am not afraid, for God is with me. I was born for this!"

May the Lord grant us many holy marriages and families, many holy priests, and many holy deacons, so that we may receive His abundant grace and be united with Our Lord, now and forever.

Remaining your humble father and servant,

Most Reverend Joseph E. Strickland
Bishop of Tyler, Texas

Our Humanity, Rooted in God

September 26, 2023

My Dear Sons and Daughters in Christ:

I write to you today to discuss more fully the fourth basic truth that I spoke of in my first pastoral letter issued on August 22, 2023, and to ask that we reflect more deeply on this important truth of our faith: "Every human person is created in the image and likeness of God, male or female, and all people should be helped to discover their true identities as children of God, and not supported in a disordered attempt to reject their undeniable biological and God-given identity."

The reality that the human community is losing this thread of truth is one of the most surprising and devastating trends of our time. The confusion and the harm that come from forsaking our biological and God-given identity are rooted in the modern tendency to deny the sovereignty of God, and for many, to deny even His very existence—thereby making ourselves into 'gods' in our own minds. This denial of the true God is demonstrated in dramatic ways as we begin to lose the thread of who we are. To answer the basic question of our identity, we must turn to God and to the truth He has revealed to us. When we attempt to answer this question of who we are without first seeking an answer from God, we find ourselves immersed in the chaos which we see around us today. Thankfully, God has revealed a beautiful picture of who we are, and Sacred Scripture and the Sacred Tradition of our Catholic faith offer much to help us paint the wondrous picture of the human person. "So, God created man in his own image, in the image of God he created him; male and female he created them." (Gen 1:27).

The truth that God has created us in His own image and likeness takes us beyond the natural level to the supernatural destiny that we all share. As the Catechism of the Catholic Church states, "The human body shares in the dignity of 'the image of God': it is a human body precisely because it is animated by a spiritual soul, and it is the whole human person that is intended to become, in the body of Christ, a temple of the Spirit." (CCC 364-365).

In his Apostolic Exhortation *Christifideles Laici,* St. John Paul II wrote about an "anthropological foundation for masculinity and femininity." He stated that this "is a plan that 'from the beginning' has been indelibly imprinted in the very being of the human person—men and women—and, therefore, in the make-up, meaning and deepest working of the individual." (*Christifideles Laici, December 30, 1988, para. 50*).

In today's culture there is a preoccupation with one's own identity, which speaks to a deeply held longing in the heart and soul of each person to find meaning in his or her life. We try to express in some way, through the physical reality of our lives, the stirrings we feel within our souls. Although there is a wide diversity of human experience, and although every life offers something unique and unrepeatable, we all share one simple, clear, and yet inconceivably profound truth: we are the Beloved, which means we are in a relationship with the One Who Loves. This foundational truth is what actually gives our lives the meaning we are truly seeking, if only we would embrace our true identity in God and enter into relationship with Him. We cannot and do not create our own identity—our identity comes from our Creator alone. The Catechism of the Catholic Church provides us a beautiful quotation from St. Catherine of Siena which gives us a glimpse of our identity in God's eyes. St. Catherine writes: "What made you establish man in so great a dignity? Certainly, the incalculable love by which you have looked on your creature in yourself! You are taken with love for her; for by love indeed you created her, by love you have given her a being capable of tasting your eternal Good." (CCC 356).

We see many agendas in the world today that relate to human identity, in particular "sexual identity." One that is very much before our eyes in this time is the LGBTQ agenda. As I stated in my pastoral letter from September 12, 2023: "The Church teaches that those who experience feelings of same-sex attraction or gender dysphoria do not sin simply because they have such feelings, but freely acting upon these feelings is sinful and not in accordance with God's design for His children."

Prior to his election as Pope Benedict XVI, Joseph Cardinal Ratzinger wrote: "In Genesis 3, we find that this truth about persons being an image of God has been obscured by original sin. There inevitably follows a loss of awareness of the covenantal character of the union these people had with God and with each other. The human body retains its 'spousal significance' but this is now clouded by sin. Thus, in Genesis 19:1-11, the deterioration due to sin continues in the story of the men of Sodom. There can be no doubt of the moral judgement made there against homosexual relations." (Joseph Cardinal Ratzinger, *Letter to the Bishops of the Catholic Church on the Pastoral Care of Homosexual Persons*, October 1986, para. 6).

Cardinal Ratzinger continued: "To choose someone of the same sex for one's sexual activity is to annul the rich symbolism and meaning, not to mention the goals, of the Creator's sexual design. Homosexual activity is not a complementary union, able to transmit life, and so it thwarts the call to a life of that form of self-giving which the Gospel says is the essence of Christian living. This does not mean that homosexual persons are not often generous and giving of themselves; but when they engage in homosexual activity, they confirm within themselves a disordered sexual inclination which is essentially self-indulgent." (Joseph Cardinal Ratzinger, *Letter to the Bishops of the Catholic Church on the Pastoral Care of Homosexual Persons*, October 1986, para. 7).

We must be loving but clear, therefore, that those who carry the burden of same-sex attraction must not act upon these inclinations because such activities are contrary to the biological and God-given identity of the individual, and therefore contrary to the will of God in all cases. We as their clergy, family, and friends must surround these individuals with love and support so they may embrace their crosses and live out their authentic, God-given identity.

The transgender movement is another face of the LGBTQ agenda, and it is also at odds with the Catholic understanding of the human being. This movement seeks to fundamentally alter the way our world views the biological and God-given identity of each person. A rapidly increasing number of young people are being caught up in the transgender movement in these times rather than being told the truth of who they are as a beloved child of God. We can certainly acknowledge that there are complex reasons why a person may have feelings of gender dysphoria, but it is important for each person to understand that regardless of feelings, a person's biological identity is given by God, and it is unchangeable by man. Parents should not be afraid to address the falsehood of gender ideology with their children in an age-appropriate manner, and parents should also reinforce the fact that although hormones and surgeries might change one's appearance, those medical procedures cannot change the sex of even one cell of the body.

Many who support the agenda of "transgenderism" would state that when a biological male identifies as a female and has "gender reassignment," this is in actuality a "gender confirmation" as his anatomy now reflects his "true gender." The Catechism states, however, that: "The unity of soul and body is so profound that one has to consider the soul to be the 'form' of the body: i.e., it is because of its spiritual soul that the body made of matter becomes a living, human body; spirit and matter, in man, are not two natures united, but rather their union forms a single nature." (CCC 365). And also, "Man and woman have been created, which is to say, willed by God: on the one hand, in perfect equality as human persons; on the other, in their respective beings as man and woman. 'Being man' or 'being woman' is a reality which is good and willed by God ...." (CCC 369). Therefore, transition surgeries or elective medical treatment given for the purpose of attempting to "transition" a person to a gender other than his or her God-given biological sex are gravely evil. (Note: There are rare medical cases of intersex individuals who have been born with an unclear biological sex or both male and female characteristics. These cases are beyond the scope of this pastoral letter and should be addressed with your pastor and medical team.)

It is important to note here that we must ALWAYS, ALWAYS treat all people with respect, compassion, and recognition of their intrinsic dignity. Therefore, men and women with homosexual tendencies or with gender dysphoria must be treated with love and compassion and should always be respected as the precious children of God that they are. This includes telling them the truth in charity.

All of this brings us to the upcoming Synod on Synodality which is emerging as an attempt by some to change the focus of Catholicism from eternal salvation of souls in Christ, to making every person feel affirmed regardless of what choices they have made or will make in life. One of the topics that reportedly will be discussed during the Synod is the blessing of same-sex relationships. Archbishop Victor Manuel Fernandez, Prefect of the Dicastery for the Doctrine of the Faith, stated in July 2023, when asked about blessings for homosexual couples: "If a blessing is given in such a way that it does not cause that confusion, it will have to be analyzed and confirmed." However, we must look to the perennial and unchanging teaching of the Church—such a blessing would not be licit and, therefore, would undoubtedly cause confusion. In fact, the very same office, the Congregation (now Dicastery) for the Doctrine of the Faith, released a statement on March 15, 2021, entitled *Responsum of the Congregation for the Doctrine of the Faith to a dubium regarding the blessing of the unions of persons of the same sex.* In this Responsum, the previous Prefect of the Congregation, Luis Cardinal Ladaria, stated that God "does not and cannot bless sin" and that, "For the above mentioned reasons, the Church does not have, and cannot have, the power to bless unions of persons of the same sex in the sense intended above." Because truth cannot change, we must acknowledge that the Dicastery cannot come to a different conclusion now which would overturn the original statement of truth from the same office. Truth is based on God's Divine Word as revealed in Sacred Scripture and Sacred Tradition, and as guarded by the Magisterium of the Church. Therefore, any attempt to permit blessings of same-sex unions would be an attack upon the Sacred Deposit of Faith.

Additionally, the Responsum also stated the following: "Blessings belong to the category of the sacramentals, whereby the Church 'calls us to praise God, encourages us to implore his protection, and exhorts us to seek his mercy by our holiness of life.' In addition, they 'have been established as a kind of imitation of the sacraments, blessings are signs above all of spiritual effects that are achieved through the Church's intercession.' Consequently, in order to conform with the nature of sacramentals, when a blessing is invoked on particular human relationships, in addition to the right intention of those who participate, it is necessary that what is blessed be objectively and positively ordered to receive and express grace, according to the designs of God inscribed in creation, and fully revealed by Christ the Lord. Therefore, only those realities which are in themselves ordered to serve those ends are congruent with the essence of the blessing imparted by the Church. For this reason, it is not licit to impart a blessing on relationships, or partnerships, even stable, that involve sexual activity outside of marriage (i.e., outside the indissoluble union of a man and a woman open in itself to the transmission of life), as is the case of the unions between persons of the same sex. The presence in such relationships of positive elements, which are in themselves to be valued and appreciated, cannot justify these relationships and render them legitimate objects of an ecclesial blessing, since the positive elements exist within the context of a union not ordered to the Creator's plan." (*Responsum of the Congregation for the Doctrine of the Faith to a dubium regarding the blessing of the unions of persons of the same sex,* March 15, 2021).

I want to reiterate that this is not an attempt in any way to discriminate against those who carry the burden of same-sex attraction, but rather it is a reminder of the truth of the liturgical rite and of the nature of the sacramentals. We cannot honor God who is truth by attempting to offer blessings which run counter to His truth.

In closing, I would like to say to those with same-sex attraction or gender dysphoria, Christ loves you and the Catholic Church welcomes you. We are all struggling to grow in holiness. I invite you to come and sit with us, pray with us, worship with us, and experience the overwhelming power of God's love and mercy with us. The truth is, at the core of our existence is Love, and there is no power in Heaven or on Earth that can keep the Father, Son, and Holy Spirit from loving us fully and completely. We are invited at every moment to embrace the love that God offers us, but in His infinite wisdom and goodness He does not force Himself upon us. Love is a choice, and it is always a sacrifice, but it is a sacrifice He first made for us, and it is a choice He is calling us to make for Him. Let the scales fall from our eyes that we may get a glimpse of how much Our Father loves us as His Beloved and run to Him always as the source of our ultimate fulfillment. "Fear not, for I have redeemed you; I have called you by name, you are mine." (Isaiah 43:1).

May the Lord bless you and may you find your true identity in the abundance of His boundless love.

Remaining your humble father and servant,

Most Reverend Joseph E. Strickland
Bishop of Tyler, Texas

Human Love in the Divine Plan

October 3, 2023

My Dear Sons and Daughters in Christ,

As we continue to review important truths of our Catholic faith, I am writing to you today to address the fifth truth in my Pastoral Letter of August 22, 2023: "Sexual activity outside marriage is always gravely sinful and cannot be condoned, blessed, or deemed permissible by any authority inside the Church."

Human sexuality is a beautiful gift from God and is woven into the being of each man and each woman. Every person is created in the image of God, and all people—both married and single—are called to chastity and to live out God's divine plan for their lives. "The chaste person maintains the integrity of the powers of life and love placed in him. This integrity ensures the unity of the person; it is opposed to any behavior that would impair it." (CCC 2338). God's plan for our sexual nature is this—that we abstain from sex before marriage, and that we are faithful to our partner within marriage; or if single, that we are celibate (not engaging in sexual relations). This is God's plan for us because He loves us so much and wants the best for us, and He has given us the awesome power to be participants with Him in bringing forth new life. This is a tremendous gift which also carries with it tremendous responsibilities. If this gift is misused, it can lead to much sorrow and human suffering. Conversely, if this gift is used properly, it leads to much joy, and to strong and healthy families which build up society and bring glory to God.

Christian marriage is a sacrament in which God pours out His grace upon the married couple so they may grow together so profoundly that the two become united together as a new, single creation. "But from the beginning of creation, God made them male and female. For this reason, a man shall leave his father and mother [and be joined to his wife], and the two shall become one flesh. So, they are no longer two but one flesh. Therefore, what God has joined together, no human being must separate." (Mk 10:6-9). The husband and wife are called to a mutually exclusive union, open to the gift of new life. So just as they are no longer two, but one flesh—when the husband and wife come together in the conjugal embrace, they have the potential to bring forth new life wherein the two of them quite literally have become one flesh in their offspring. "God blessed them, and God said to them: 'Be fertile and multiply; fill the earth and subdue it.'" (Gen 1:28). The gift of human sexuality is to be lived within the bonds of marriage even if the couple is not able to bear children. Pope St. John Paul II stated regarding couples without children, "You are no less loved by God; your love for each other is complete and fruitful when it is open to others, to the needs of the apostolate, to the needs of the poor, to the needs of orphans, to the needs of the world." (St Pope John Paul II, Homily; February 13, 1982).

This basic truth of morality—that human sexuality is ordered towards a lifelong, mutually exclusive union open to the gift of new life—must be recovered for the sake of humanity. The so-called sexual revolution that blossomed in the 1960's has overtaken human society in devastating ways. Many have accused the Catholic Church of focusing too much on sexual morality, but if we look at our present landscape, it seems evident that we, the shepherds, have failed to focus enough on this gravely important issue. Instead of having an understanding of the importance of living a chaste life, humanity seems to be caught up in an "anything goes" mentality regarding sexual activity. Furthermore, rather than the focus being on God's creative plan for life through a man and woman in a committed and sacramental marriage open to children, the focus seems often to be only about sexual pleasure even if it departs completely from God's plan, and even if it erodes the dignity of the human person.

This distorted understanding of our sexual nature—one in which human relationships are understood on a transactional level with a so-called "hook-up" culture, widespread and easy divorce, easy availability of contraception and abortion, and deviant sexual practices—seeks to reduce relationships to what one person can take from another, denigrating the dignity and sanctity of the human person, and leaving its participants feeling empty and unfulfilled. Sexual sins are discussed and glorified, even on social media, as casually as though one were discussing the weather.

One of the necessary elements of recovering a healthy understanding of human sexuality is to regain an understanding of the fact that our sexual nature is a beautiful gift from God. The fact that God has created us male and female and established a complementarity between the sexes is truly one of God's most profound blessings. Pope St John Paul II beautifully explained this in his teachings called *The Theology of the Body: Human Love in the Divine Plan*. These teachings are a reflection on this profound gift, and on the fact that human beings, who are made in the image of God, are made for self-giving love, not self-getting love. In an Apostolic Letter, St. John Paul II explained that man and woman exist not only "side by side" or "together," but also exist mutually "one for the other." (Mulieris Dignitatem, para. 7).

The Catechism of the Catholic Church states: "'The intimate community of life and love which constitutes the married state has been established by the Creator and endowed by him with its own proper laws … God himself is the author of marriage.' The vocation to marriage is written in the very nature of man and woman as they came from the hand of the Creator. Marriage is not a purely human institution despite the many variations it may have undergone through the centuries in different cultures, social structures, and spiritual attitudes. These differences should not cause us to forget its common and permanent characteristics. Although the dignity of this institution is not transparent everywhere with the same clarity, some sense of the greatness of the matrimonial union exists in all cultures. 'The well-being of the individual person and of both human and Christian society is closely bound up with the healthy state of conjugal and family life.'" (CCC 1603).

We must also reclaim the concept of covenant which is so prevalent throughout both the Old and New Testament. Simply put, a covenant is an exchange of persons – "I am yours, and you are mine" – and is an important part of the creation of a family unit. In marriage, the man and the woman give of themselves entirely to the other, being open to the begetting of new life. Pleasure is a component of sexual relations, but it is not the only component; sexual relations as designed and intended by God also entail openness to new life and a lifelong, unbreakable bond between a man and a woman. If a couple, regardless of who they are, enter into a sexual relationship without intending that relationship to be faithful, exclusive, and open to new life (all of which is what the sacrament of Matrimony is intended to foster), then they are engaging in only an imitation of true love which is gravely sinful, and which ultimately deviates from the happiness, joy, and fulfillment that God truly desires for His children.

When the so-called sexual revolution began in the 1960's, with a movement towards sexual expression no longer being confined to marriage, many greeted it as a doorway into unfettered freedom, but what this freedom actually looked like was epidemics of sexually transmitted diseases, tens of millions of abortions, rampant pornography, increase in rape and child abuse, and devastating effects on the family and marriage. And yet, still we hear the cry—that the thing human beings really need is more freedom.

It is estimated that over 40% of all couples in the U.S. now live together unwed, as opposed to being married. We are sure that we have "made progress" because we are now so "free." However, most people misunderstand the true nature of freedom. As St. John Paul II once stated so eloquently, "Freedom consists not in doing what we like, but in having the right to do what we ought." As our society moves further away from truth and from God's design for families, we will inevitably destroy the very foundation of the society in which we live. Many fail to see that if a society which is built on God's truth dies, individual freedoms will die along with it. The destruction of marriage and the family lead to the death of the society, and even more profoundly, to the loss of so many souls who participate in this self-destruction. This is why the Blessed Mother, Our Lady of Fatima, warned Venerable Sister Lucia dos Santos that "the decisive battle between the kingdom of Christ and Satan will be over marriage and the family."

As we discuss the extreme importance of marriage and the family, I would also like us to turn our attention to the most tragic fruit of the sexual revolution—abortion—the gravely serious sin of murdering our children. Abortion is the termination of a pregnancy by removal or expulsion of an embryo or fetus (a living child) from the uterus, resulting in the child's death. The Catechism of the Catholic Church states: "Human life must be respected and protected absolutely from the moment of conception. From the first moment of his existence, a human being must be recognized as having the rights of a person—among which is the inviolable right of every innocent being to life." (CCC 2270). And yet many demand the "freedom" of being allowed to abort their child.

According to the World Health Organization (WHO), every year in the world there are a staggering 73 million induced abortions. This corresponds to approximately 200,000 abortions per day worldwide. In the U.S. alone, the Guttmacher Institute reports 930,160 abortions were performed in 2020, a rate of more than 2,500 abortions per day. This is almost one million American children killed in the womb each year before they are even allowed to take their first breath. There can be no greater or more tragic example of the complete breakdown of marriages and families than this, and this is why abortion is the pre-eminent issue that the Church faces today.

After the birth control pill came into being in the mid-1960's, birth-control advocacy groups such as Planned Parenthood and others claimed that there would be a decrease in abortions, as women could now engage in sexual activity with a greatly reduced chance of pregnancy. Instead, the connection between higher contraceptive use and an increase in the number of abortions has now been firmly established. In 1981, abortion advocate Dr. Christopher Tietze wrote: "A high correlation between abortion experience and contraceptive experience can be expected in populations to which both contraception and abortion are available … Women who have practiced contraception are more likely to have had abortions than those who have not practiced contraception, and women who have had abortions are more likely to have been contraceptors than women without a history of abortion." (Dr. Christopher Tietze: "Abortion and Contraception." *Abortion: Readings and Research.* Butterworth & Company, Toronto, Canada 1981, pages 54 to 60.) The conclusion which has now been made manifest by decades of data is that the use of contraceptives encourages more sexual activity outside of marriage, and when contraceptives fail, women turn to abortion as a remedy.

At the National Prayer Breakfast in Washington, D.C, on February 5, 1994, St. Teresa of Calcutta prophetically stated, "Once that living love is destroyed by contraception, abortion follows easily … And abortion, which often follows from contraception, brings a people to be spiritually poor, and that is the worst poverty and the most difficult to overcome."

As we approach the beginning of the Synod on Synodality, it is important for us to remember and embrace the profound sacredness of the conjugal union between husband and wife, and the truth that sexual activity outside of marriage is always gravely sinful and cannot be condoned, blessed, or deemed permissible by any authority inside the Church. God calls us to stand firm and reject any path that deviates from His truth, so let us be on guard against any who would attempt to condone, bless, or encourage such activity, as this would be opposed to Christ, to His Church, and to the Sacred Deposit of Faith. We must remember that God's divine truth can never change, and neither God nor the Church can cooperate with or bless sin.

In conclusion, it is a fact that we as a society have become all too familiar with a long list of sexual sins including fornication, adultery, contraception, sodomy, masturbation, pornography, and many other forms of unchastity that are so prevalent today. The call to sexual continence is a struggle for many, and it certainly runs contrary to the tide of our current culture which revels in unchastity. However, the Church points us to the truth that human sexuality is a beautiful gift from God which is intended to draw us closer into Him as we commit to live a holy and chaste life. We should look to the examples of saints, both married and single, who embraced holy and chaste lives so that we may see that not only is it possible to live lives in accordance with God's plan for chastity, but it is essential to do so in order to find the true joy that comes with fulfilling God's call for our lives.

We should also see that the devastation and dire spiritual poverty that we see in society from the forsaking of His truth stand in stark contrast to the profound beauty of God's plan for us if we would embrace His divine will regarding our authentic human sexual identity. We must open our hearts and our minds to Christ's message—that the road to salvation is narrow, and the road to perdition is broad. "Enter by the narrow gate, since the road that leads to destruction is wide and spacious, and many take it; but it is a narrow gate and a hard road that leads to life, and only a few find it." (Matt 7:13-14). Christ shows us how to give of ourselves entirely for the sake of the beloved—to die to oneself, to sacrifice— as He did on the cross for His bride, the Church. When we or our loved ones wander into lust and sin, we should never despair, but instead throw ourselves at the merciful feet of Almighty God. Let us always remember that God's mercy is ever-present if only we will repent and seek His forgiveness.

May Almighty God bless you, and may we rejoice in the mystery and the God-given gift of our sexual nature as we strive to conform ourselves in humility to God's plan of love for our lives.

Remaining your humble father and servant,

Most Reverend Joseph E. Strickland
Bishop of Tyler, Texas

The Error of Universalism

October 10, 2023

My Dear Sons and Daughters in Christ,

It is an honor and a joy to continue to share the basic truths of our Catholic faith with you, as we now delve more deeply into the sixth truth I outlined in my Pastoral Letter of August 22, 2023: "The belief that all men and women will be saved regardless of how they live their lives (a concept commonly referred to as universalism) is false and is dangerous, as it contradicts what Jesus tells us repeatedly in the Gospel. Jesus says we must 'deny ourselves, take up our cross and follow Him.' (Matt 16:24). He has given us the way, through His grace, to victory over sin and death through repentance and sacramental confession. It is essential that we embrace the joy and hope, as well as the freedom, that come from repentance and humbly confessing our sins. Through repentance and sacramental confession, every battle with temptation and sin can be a small victory that leads us to embrace the great victory that Christ has won for us." We are all sinners, and we are all in need of a Savior because we are all born into original sin and, therefore, subject to its consequences. (cf. Rom 5:12-21). Original sin was the first sin that was committed by our first parents, Adam and Eve, in disobedience of God. That original sin is now a hereditary stain with which we are all born on account of our descent from Adam and Eve. Thus, original sin is an ongoing privation of God's grace, and because of its effect in our lives, we as humans are born in a state of separation from God. If we were left in this state of original sin, we would be eternally separated from God because nothing unclean will be allowed to enter into Heaven. (cf. Rev 21:27). However, through Baptism, God has made a way for us to be justified in Him—through Jesus Christ alone—and to remove not only the stain of the original sin of our first parents which we carry, but also the stain of all actual sins we ourselves commit. And for our sins after we have been baptized, God has given us the Sacrament of Reconciliation (also called Confession or Penance) in order to allow us to repent and be cleansed of the stain of our sins.

From the Catechism of the Catholic Church, we read that "Sin is an offense against God: 'Against you, you alone, have I sinned, and done that which is evil in your sight.' Sin sets itself against God's love for us and turns our hearts away from it. Like the first sin, it is disobedience, a revolt against God through the will to become 'like gods,' knowing and determining good and evil. Sin is thus 'love of oneself even to contempt of God.' In this proud self-exaltation, sin is diametrically opposed to the obedience of Jesus, which achieves our salvation." (CCC 1850).

That first sentence is packed with deep theological insight – "Sin is an offense against God." Consider that God is infinitely good and holy, and He is infinite love. Thus, according to St. Thomas Aquinas in his Summa Theologica, when we sin, we sin against the infinite, and thus our sins are infinitely offensive to Him. "Now a sin which is committed against God is infinite: because the gravity of a sin increases according to the greatness of the person sinned against (thus it is a more grievous sin to strike the sovereign than a private individual) and God's greatness is infinite. Therefore, an infinite punishment is due for a sin committed against God." (Summa Theologica; I-II, q.87, a. 4, obj. 2).

In our current society which is so afflicted with the errors of moral relativism, the temptation is all too strong to look at the weight of sin from a human perspective rather than from the divine perspective. We make excuses for our sins, explaining that the things we do are "not all that bad." Further, the temptation exists to presume upon the mercy of God, assuming that surely a loving and merciful God will overlook our disobedience and failures even if we do not seek forgiveness because He is infinitely merciful. This line of thinking sometimes progresses to our assuming that salvation will ultimately be offered to all people simply because God is infinitely merciful, and therefore all men will be saved. This is the error of universalism. This error could lead one to ask, "What then is the point of conversion of heart to Jesus Christ? Why bother following Christ at all?" This is extremely dangerous, as it prevents us from seeing the need for true and authentic repentance. It is a deadly indifference that imperils our immortal souls and puts us at eternal risk of separation from God. "For the wages of sin is death, but the gift of God is eternal life in Christ Jesus our Lord." (Rom 6:23). Although God does make an accommodation for our weak and fallen human nature, that accommodation is through the sacraments of Baptism and Reconciliation (sacramental confession) which move us into a right relationship with Our Savior Jesus Christ, through whom alone our salvation comes.

Sin damages our relationship with God and cuts us off from sharing in His life of grace, and we cannot restore this life of grace ourselves as we are finite beings with only finite capabilities, and the One whom we have offended through sin is infinite. We are not capable of making infinite reparations. Thus, we can only reestablish a life of grace through the One who is infinite. He alone is capable of restoring life.

"When the disciples heard this, they were greatly astonished and said, 'Who then can be saved?' Jesus looked at them and said, 'For human beings this is impossible, but for God all things are possible.'" (Matt 19:25-26). Salvation comes by Jesus alone (c.f. Acts 4:12). The saving grace that Jesus Christ won for us on the cross is a free gift from God that man receives through repentance, faith, and baptism. Once we are baptized into Christ, it is through repentance and sacramental confession that every battle with temptation and sin can be a small victory that leads us to embrace the great victory that Christ has won for us.

A key word I would like us to reflect on in this discussion is "metanoia." This Greek word means "change in one's way of life resulting from penitence or spiritual conversion." This change lies at the heart of what it means to be a disciple of Jesus Christ, and while it involves an initial choice to turn around and follow Christ, metanoia actually denotes a way of life that seeks constant change to follow Jesus Christ more fully and more profoundly. Many of the stories of the greatest saints involve a profound metanoia: St. Augustine, St. Ignatius of Loyola, St. Francis of Assisi, St. Mary Magdalene and St. Theresa Benedicta, to name only a few. Their stories involve a dramatic turn from sin and a clear choice to be forever changed and to follow Jesus Christ. The drama of their moments of conversion are then followed by a lifetime of turning more fully to the Sacred Heart of Jesus, and more completely away from sin.

Now that we have examined the great danger in universalism—and in denying that the price of sin is eternal separation from God unless we embrace the call to repentance of sin and living in the Way of Jesus Christ—how do we move into the joy and the hope, as well as the freedom, that comes from true repentance and turning to Christ? In the simplest of terms, the answer to how we go about this is to live out our Catholic faith in Word and Sacrament. The Word of God contained in the Sacred Scriptures nurtures us throughout this journey and points us always to truth; and the sacraments—instituted by Christ Himself—offer us encounters with God's grace that strengthen us along the way, changing us from sinner to saved.

As we deepen our understanding of the sacraments, and in particular the sacraments of Baptism, Confirmation, and Reconciliation (also called Confession or Penance), we are drawn more deeply into the metanoia we are all called to embrace. These three sacraments in particular build on one another as our relationship with Jesus Christ grows. While the Church acknowledges that God is sovereign and therefore, He is not bound to dispensing His grace through the sacraments alone, we recognize that the sacraments are essential for the Christian life and are the ordinary means that God has given to us so that we may receive sanctifying grace and the salvation He won for us on the cross.

Baptism of course is the necessary sacrament of our initial repentance, conversion, and incorporation into the Christian life. It frees us from original sin and gives us sanctifying grace, allowing us to share in His life and love. A beautiful and essential element of the Church's teaching is the indelible (permanent) character that Baptism confers on a person; one can never be unbaptized. In the Nicene Creed we recite at mass, we confess "one Baptism for the forgiveness of sins." The great consolation here is that once configured to Christ, we can always return to Him no matter how far we have wandered away in our sinfulness, if only we repent and confess our sins. Thus, Baptism permanently configures us to Christ and gives us the grace to live this new relationship.

Confirmation is most profoundly a strengthening of the original gift of life in the Holy Spirit that we receive at Baptism. Pentecost as described in the Acts of the Apostles can be understood as the Confirmation of the Apostles in the Holy Spirit, and we can see clearly the spiritual strength they received as they formed the Church in Her beginnings. We are blessed with the very same gifts of the Holy Spirit when we are confirmed, and this sacrament gives us the strength to constantly turn from sin and grow closer to the Sacred Heart of Christ.

Finally, the Sacrament of Reconciliation (or Confession or Penance) can be described as the sacrament of continuing metanoia. We all stumble in sinfulness and are called to humbly confess our sins and strive for deeper holiness. In our ongoing journey of faith, the Sacrament of Reconciliation is of critical importance, and we all need to understand that it is a loving encounter with the same Jesus Christ who we receive in the Eucharist. The beauty of this sacrament is that it expresses God's abundant mercy and emphasizes that He never "takes pleasure in the death of the wicked" but constantly gives them the opportunity to "turn from their ways and live." (Ezek 33:11). As the Catechism states: "Those who approach the sacrament of Penance obtain pardon from God's mercy for the offense committed against him, and are, at the same time, reconciled with the Church which they have wounded by their sins and which by charity, by example, and by prayer labors for their conversion." (CCC 1422).

As we face the challenges in the world and the Church today—and in particular with the confusion of the Synod on Synodality raging even as I write this—let us be reminded that there is only one way to eternal life: "Jesus said to him, 'I am the way and the truth and the life. No one comes to the Father except through me.'" (Jn 14:6). Our Lord also tells us plainly that not all will be saved: "Not everyone who says to me, 'Lord, Lord', will enter the kingdom of heaven, but only the one who does the will of my Father in heaven." (Matt 7:21). Therefore, it is imperative that we remain firmly anchored to the Sacred Deposit of Faith and reject any idea which would deviate from the perennial teachings of the Catholic Church.

This includes any who—in the name of ecumenism or dialogue—would promote the error of universalism or attempt to offer a way of salvation other than through Jesus Christ and His Church. The tragic temptation to eviscerate the meaning of His Life through a so-called universalism that renders Him meaningless is a great manifestation of the evil we face today. Let us reject the notion that all are saved with no need for metanoia, and instead embrace the wondrous metanoia God offers us only through His Son. We have been given the greatest and most precious gift imaginable; let us recognize that gift and share it with a world that is so desperately in need of Jesus Christ, our Lord and Savior!

In conclusion, let us rejoice and be glad, because God loves us and calls us to Himself. He built a bridge in the shape of a cross so that our sin would not keep us separated from Him, and He gave us the Sacraments of Baptism, Confirmation, and Reconciliation so that we may cross that bridge and be adopted into the family of God. Jesus Christ, the Son of God, was conceived in the womb of the Blessed Virgin Mary, was born in Bethlehem, lived and taught among us, suffered and died for us, and rose from the dead. He did all of this to free us from sin and death, and to offer us the opportunity to gain everlasting life with God— Father, Son, and Holy Spirit. That is the Good News, and we must joyfully share it with the world!

May Almighty God bless you, my brothers and sisters, and may we continue to grow stronger in faith and turn our hearts always to Jesus Christ who is our salvation.

Remaining your humble father and servant,

Most Reverend Joseph E. Strickland
Bishop of Tyler

Lift High the Cross

October 17, 2023

My Dear Sons and Daughters in Christ,

It has been an honor and a joy to share some basic and essential truths of the Catholic faith with you through this series of Pastoral Letters. Today I would like to discuss the seventh and final truth that I listed in my Pastoral Letter of August 22, 2023:

"In order to follow Jesus Christ, we must willingly choose to take up our cross instead of attempting to avoid the cross and suffering that Our Lord offers to each of us individually in our daily lives. The mystery of redemptive suffering— i.e. suffering that Our Lord allows us to experience and accept in this world and then offer back to Him in union with His suffering—humbles us, purifies us, and draws us deeper into the joy of a life lived in Christ. That is not to say that we must enjoy or seek out suffering, but if we are united to Christ, as we experience our daily sufferings, we can find the hope and joy that exist amidst the suffering and persevere to the end in all our suffering. (cf. 2 Tim 4:6-8)."

The question of why suffering is woven into our human existence has preoccupied and perplexed humanity since the dawn of history. Suffering seems to be a great mystery, and when we are in the midst of it, we might ask, "Why does it have to be this way? Why does God allow us to suffer if He loves us?" The ultimate answer to these questions is this—free will. God created us, He loves us, and He wants the very best for us in every way; He wants us to live forever in Heaven with Him in a loving relationship. However, to be in an eternal, loving relationship with Him, we have to accept His love and then choose to love Him back because love is only possible if one has a choice to love or not to love. God, who is love, will not force us to love Him and spend eternity with Him against our will because that would not be love.

Our first parents, Adam and Eve, chose to disobey God—an act contrary to love—and thereby sin and death were introduced into the world. As the Catechism of the Catholic Church states: "Man, tempted by the devil, let his trust in his Creator die in his heart and, abusing his freedom, disobeyed God's command. This is what man's first sin consisted of. All subsequent sin would be disobedience toward God and lack of trust in his goodness." (CCC 397).

However, God sent a new Adam—His Divine Son, Jesus—to redeem us from both the original sin committed by our first parents, as well as the personal sin we each commit in our own lives through our thoughts, words, deeds, and omissions. This act of perfect sacrifice by Jesus Christ on the cross shows us the model of how suffering can be redemptive, and it forms the basis for a concept the Church knows as the Economy of Salvation, whereby we recognize God's activity in governing the world, particularly regarding our salvation won by Christ. When we embrace the mystery of suffering in God's Economy of Salvation, and when we come to recognize that our pain is actually an invitation to participate with Christ on the cross, we find not only meaning, but even a profound beauty in suffering as it humbles us, purifies us, and conforms us to Christ in a way nothing else could. It can oftentimes be difficult for us to recognize the good that comes from suffering when we are undergoing it, but it is typically in those times of suffering when God is refining us the most.

It is important for us to recognize in our suffering that God's will for us always includes mercy, and that trust in God involves believing He loves us perfectly, and that He has compassion for us. However, this can be difficult to realize and accept, especially when there seems to be no relief of the pain, no healing from disease, etc. However, when God provided the ultimate sacrifice, His Divine Son, this sacrifice covered the whole world with His compassion and His mercy. The suffering of Christ on the cross—our sign of hope and of eternal life—allows us the opportunity to enter into that hope and that promise by uniting our suffering with His, and to recognize that within our pain and suffering can be found the immense compassion and mercy of God.

How, though, can our suffering become redemptive? The Catechism of the Catholic Church teaches that all suffering "can also have a redemptive meaning for the sins of others" if we unite it to Christ's passion. (CCC 1502). "… Christ not only allows himself to be touched by the sick, but he makes their miseries his own … By his passion and death on the cross Christ has given a new meaning to suffering: it can henceforth configure us to him and unite us with his redemptive Passion." (CCC 1505). Suffering in union with the passion of Christ "acquires a new meaning; it becomes a participation in the saving work of Jesus." (CCC 1521).

Redemptive suffering is a beautiful and perfect love. We are able to suffer redemptively only through the grace of Christ. You might sometimes hear Catholics say about suffering – "offer it up." That is because suffering can have a purpose when it is united with Christ on the cross. It can bring much hope and joy into your life even in the midst of suffering to know that something beautiful is being brought about from something difficult. The important thing to realize is that redemptive suffering is not something you go through alone—Christ is with you, experiencing it with you! In our suffering which is offered to Christ, He draws us into Himself and into His Sacred Heart.

"Offering it up" transforms suffering from misery into love. However, when someone is in the midst of deep suffering, it can sound dismissive to tell them to "offer it up." We must be empathetic to those who suffer, for it is sometimes difficult to see how suffering can be redemptive when one is in the midst of terrible suffering, or if a child or a loved one is suffering. However, we can pray not only to offer up our own sufferings for the sake of others, but we can pray also that the Lord will use the sufferings of others for their own purification and spiritual growth, even if they cannot see to do so themselves. All suffering, when united with Christ's suffering, is redemptive. As St. Paul tells us, "Now I rejoice in my sufferings for your sake, and in my flesh, I am filling up what is lacking in the afflictions of Christ on behalf of his body, which is the church…" (Col 1:24). Christ's sacrifice on the cross was perfect, but what is lacking from His perfect sacrifice? Only our participation in it. Christ's perfect sacrifice on the cross destroyed death and the eternal effects of sin. And in our suffering, united with His, He gives us the power to participate in the salvation He won for us.

Suffering can bring a profound loneliness at times. However, it is this loneliness which can cause us to reach out, past earthly comfort, to the One who calls us to participate in the mystery of suffering with Him. Jesus chose to enter into our loneliness by becoming human. He experienced profound loneliness in the Garden of Gethsemane, where he underwent His agony as He prepared for His impending death, and even His disciples did not stay awake with Him. (cf.

Matt 26:36-45). On the cross Jesus cried out, "My God, my God, why have you forsaken me?" (Matt. 27:46). By His Passion, Jesus endured the ultimate loneliness in order to fill our loneliness with His presence, and in our suffering, He is profoundly present.

As disciples of Jesus Christ, we are not called to seek out suffering, but when God allows suffering to come into our lives, we are called to accept the cross He offers us and embrace the work God is performing in our souls as necessary for our purification and sanctification. Although He was sinless, Jesus gave us a perfect model to follow: "Surely, he did not help angels but rather the descendants of Abraham; therefore, he had to become like his brothers in every way, that he might be a merciful and faithful high priest before God to expiate the sins of the people. Because he himself was tested through what he suffered, he is able to help those who are being tested." (Heb 2:16-18). Jesus beautifully demonstrates this in the Garden of Gethsemane as He says, "My Father, if it is possible, let this cup pass from me; yet, not as I will, but as you will." (Matt 26:39). Many great saints throughout the ages have also embraced this essential reality of the cross in their lives and have given us an example of embracing suffering.

Pope St. John Paul II left us a beautiful apostolic letter, *Salvifici Doloris,* in which he contemplates the role of suffering in salvation history, including how Our Blessed Mother exemplifies what it means to share in Christ's suffering: "'… As a witness to her Son's Passion by her presence, and as a sharer in it by her compassion, Mary offered a unique contribution to the Gospel of suffering,' … She truly has a special title to be able to claim that she 'completes in her flesh' – as already in her heart – 'what is lacking in Christ's afflictions.'" (Salvifici Doloris, para. 25)

St. Gemma Galgani, also known as the Flower of Lucca, was a mystic who was born in 1878 in Italy. Throughout her life she had many mystical experiences. She suffered greatly, and she died of tuberculosis at age 25. She gave us this beautiful message on suffering: "Jesus once said to me, 'Do you know, daughter, for what reason I send crosses to souls dear to me? I desire to possess their souls, entirely, and for this I surround them with crosses, and I enclose them in sufferings and tribulation, that they may not escape from my hands; and for this I scatter thorns, that souls may fasten their affections upon no one, but find all content in Me alone. My daughter, if you do not feel the cross, it cannot be called a cross. Be sure that under the cross you will not be lost." (St Gemma Galgani, Letter to Monsignor Volpi)

As we have looked at some basic truths of our Catholic faith in this series of Pastoral Letters, we have seen the cooperative and complementary nature of the sacraments as part of God's Divine Economy of Salvation. We have looked at suffering in this letter; therefore, let us now turn to the sacrament of the Anointing of the Sick (sometimes referred to as Extreme Unction) as we reflect on the cross in our lives. Like all the sacraments, Anointing of the Sick shows us Christ is present in His Church; in this case, He is most present to us as our healing Lord. The very same Jesus who restored sight to the blind man, and who healed the woman with a hemorrhage is present to suffering souls through the ministry of His priests; and through those priests, Our Lord can bring healing of body, mind, and spirit in this sacrament. It is important to note, however, that although this sacrament is typically administered to those who are suffering from a serious physical condition, the most important effect of Anointing of the Sick is spiritual strengthening, spiritual healing, and forgiveness of sins which God imparts through this sacrament. Therefore, although a person who receives this sacrament may receive the grace of a physical healing if that is in alignment with God's will; the individual will always receive the invisible grace of spiritual healing, even if there are no visible signs of physical healing.

From the Catechism of the Catholic Church, we understand that: "The special grace of the sacrament of the Anointing of the Sick has as its effects: the uniting of the sick person to the passion of Christ, for his own good and that of the whole Church; the strengthening, peace, and courage to endure in a Christian manner the sufferings of illness or old age; the forgiveness of sins, if the sick person was not able to obtain it through the sacrament of Penance; the restoration of health, if it is conducive to the salvation of his soul; the preparation for passing over to eternal life." (CCC 1532). A person does not necessarily have to be close to death in order to receive the Anointing of the Sick, and this sacrament can be received as many times as is proper throughout a person's life when God's physical and/or spiritual healing is sought. For those close to death, a priest can perform a specific set of prayers and sacramental activities known as Last Rites, which include the Sacrament of the Anointing of the Sick, and typically a final Reconciliation (if possible), and a final reception of the Eucharist (if possible), which is known as Viaticum.

Before closing this discussion on suffering, I would like to state that there are many in the world who suffer for their faith because of attacks by their own government, or from others who are hostile to Christ and His Church. Our Lord walks especially close to these suffering souls. Let us pray for them constantly.

There are many, many saints who stand ready to assist them; let us pray for their intercession. However, I also want to mention, especially in this time of the Synod on Synodality, that we are in a unique time now as there are many who are suffering for their faith as they attempt to defend the Deposit of Faith due to attacks from within the Church herself. I would call on those who are being persecuted in this manner to remember that they also walk in the footprints of Jesus Christ, and that there are also many saints who have been persecuted by those in Christ's Church who should, above all, uphold His truth. Let us all stand firm and not waver and let us say with St. Ignatius of Antioch: "… Come fire and cross and grapplings with wild beasts …, wrenching of bones, hacking of limbs, crushing of my whole body, come cruel tortures of the devil to assail me. Only be it mine to attain unto Jesus Christ." (Letter from St. Ignatius to the Romans, chapter 5, verse 3).

In conclusion, Christ is our example of how to suffer, and He will teach us as we unite our sufferings to His. He promises that His grace is sufficient and available to all. He offers His divine life to us in the midst of our sufferings through the sacraments. I urge you, my dear sons and daughters in Christ— attend Mass every Sunday and Holy Day, and strive to attend daily mass as often as you can; go to confession frequently; pray the Rosary; and call upon the saints for assistance. Rejoice that we can participate in our own redemption and the redemption of the world by denying ourselves, taking up our cross, and following Him.

May Almighty God bless you, and may you receive the strengthening, healing, and perseverance Our Lord desires for you as you offer your sufferings to Him.

I remain your humble father and servant,

Most Reverend Joseph E. Strickland
Bishop of Tyler

Made in the USA
Las Vegas, NV
08 December 2023

82270082R00030